Healthy High

Protein

Chicken

Recipes

Discover The Art Of Crafting Delicious, Protein-Packed Chicken Meals That Nourish Your Body And Delight The Taste Buds

MATTHEW REYNOLDS

Disclaimer

The information provided in this book is for general informational purposes only. While every effort has been made to provide accurate and up-to-date information, the author and publisher make no representations or warranties of any kind, express or implied, about the completeness, accuracy, reliability, suitability, or availability of the information contained within this book. Any reliance you place on such information is strictly at your own risk.

Allergies: The recipes included in this book may contain a wide variety of ingredients, and some of them may be common allergens, such as nuts, soy, wheat, or others. It is crucial for readers to be aware of their own allergies and the allergies of those for whom they are preparing food. While efforts have been made to identify potential allergens in the recipes, the author and publisher cannot guarantee that allergenic ingredients are not present in trace amounts due to cross-contamination or other factors.

The author and publisher strongly recommend that readers with known food allergies exercise caution and consult with a qualified healthcare professional or allergist before preparing and consuming any recipe from this book. It is the responsibility of the reader to verify the ingredients used and to make informed decisions regarding their dietary choices.

The author and publisher shall not be held liable for any loss, damage, or injury resulting from the use or misuse of the information presented in this book, including allergic reactions. The author and publisher do not endorse any specific products, brands, or services mentioned in this book.

Medical Advice: The recipes and nutritional information provided in this book are intended for educational and illustrative purposes only. They are not meant to substitute for professional dietary, nutritional, or medical advice. Readers are encouraged to consult with a qualified healthcare or nutrition professional before making dietary or lifestyle changes, especially if they have specific dietary restrictions, allergies, or medical conditions

Loved the book? Don't forget to leave a review.

Table of Contents

Grilled Lemon Herb Chicken Breast

Summary: Delight your taste buds with Grilled Lemon Herb Chicken Breast, a protein-packed dish bursting with vibrant flavors. This recipe offers a perfect blend of grilled chicken, fresh herbs, and zesty lemon, creating a healthy and delicious meal.

Protein Content: Approximately 25 grams of protein per serving.

Ingredients:

- 1.5 lbs boneless, skinless chicken breasts

- 2 tablespoons olive oil

- 2 tablespoons fresh rosemary (chopped)

- 2 tablespoons fresh thyme leaves

- 4 cloves garlic (minced)

- Zest of 1 lemon

- Juice of 1 lemon

- Salt and black pepper to taste

Instructions:

1. In a bowl, mix olive oil, chopped rosemary, thyme, minced garlic, lemon zest, lemon juice, salt, and black pepper.

2. Season chicken breasts with the herb mixture, ensuring they are well coated.

3. Preheat the grill to medium-high heat.

4. Grill the chicken for 6-8 minutes per side or until fully cooked.

5. Let the chicken rest for a few minutes before slicing.

Essential Nutritional Information:

- Calories: 300 per serving

- Fat: 12g

- Carbohydrates: 2g

- Protein: 25g

Tips:

- Marinate the chicken for at least 30 minutes for enhanced flavor.

- Use a meat thermometer to ensure the chicken is cooked through.

Tricks:

- Grill lemon halves alongside chicken for extra charred flavor.

- Baste chicken with additional herb mixture while grilling.

Ingredient Substitutions:

- Substitute rosemary and thyme with your favorite herbs.

- Use chicken thighs for a juicier texture.

Baked Pesto Chicken Thighs

Summary: Experience the rich flavors of Baked Pesto Chicken Thighs, a dish that combines tender chicken thighs with the aromatic goodness of basil pesto. This recipe is a delightful balance of simplicity and taste.

Protein Content: Approximately 30 grams of protein per serving.

Ingredients:

- 1.5 lbs bone-in, skin-on chicken thighs

- 1 cup fresh basil leaves

- 1/2 cup grated Parmesan cheese

- 1/3 cup pine nuts

- 2 cloves garlic

- 1/2 cup olive oil

- Salt and black pepper to taste

Instructions:

1. In a food processor, combine basil leaves, Parmesan cheese, pine nuts, and garlic. Pulse until finely chopped.

2. With the processor running, slowly pour in the olive oil until a smooth pesto sauce forms.

3. Season chicken thighs with salt and black pepper.

4. Spread a generous layer of pesto over each chicken thigh, covering both sides.

5. Preheat the oven to 375°F (190°C).

6. Place pesto-coated chicken thighs in a baking dish.

7. Bake for 35-40 minutes or until the chicken reaches an internal temperature of 165°F (74°C).

Essential Nutritional Information:

- Calories: 400 per serving

- Fat: 30g

- Carbohydrates: 2g

- Protein: 30g

Tips:

- Marinate the chicken in pesto for a few hours for maximum flavor.

- Reserve some pesto for serving on the side.

Tricks:

- Toast pine nuts before adding to the pesto for a nuttier flavor.

- Broil for the last 5 minutes for a golden crust.

Ingredient Substitutions:

- Substitute pine nuts with almonds or walnuts.

- Use store-bought pesto for a quicker option.

Mediterranean Chicken Skewers

Summary: Embark on a culinary journey with Mediterranean Chicken Skewers. Marinated in olive oil, lemon, and aromatic herbs, these skewers offer a taste of the Mediterranean in every juicy bite.

Protein Content: Approximately 20 grams of protein per serving.

Ingredients:

- 1.5 lbs boneless, skinless chicken thighs (cut into chunks)

- 1/4 cup olive oil

- 2 tablespoons lemon juice

- 2 teaspoons dried oregano

- 2 cloves garlic (minced)

- Salt and black pepper to taste

Instructions:

1. In a bowl, whisk together olive oil, lemon juice, dried oregano, minced garlic, salt, and black pepper to create the marinade.

2. Thread chicken chunks onto skewers and place them in a shallow dish.

3. Pour the marinade over the chicken skewers, ensuring they are well coated. Marinate for at least 30 minutes.

4. Preheat the grill to medium-high heat.

5. Grill the chicken skewers for 5-7 minutes per side or until fully cooked.

Essential Nutritional Information:

- Calories: 280 per serving

- Fat: 15g

- Carbohydrates: 3g

- Protein: 20g

Tips:

- Soak wooden skewers in water before threading to prevent burning.

- Add a pinch of red pepper flakes for a hint of heat.

Tricks:

- Grill pita bread for a few seconds on each side for a warm and smoky flavor.

- Serve with a side of Greek salad for a complete meal.

Ingredient Substitutions:

- Substitute chicken thighs with chicken breast or lamb.

- Use dried rosemary if fresh oregano is unavailable.

Lemon Garlic Roast Chicken

Summary: Indulge in the classic flavors of Lemon Garlic Roast Chicken, a timeless dish featuring a whole chicken infused with the freshness of lemon and the savory notes of garlic. This roast is sure to be a crowd-pleaser.

Protein Content: Approximately 25 grams of protein per serving.

Ingredients:

- 1 whole chicken (about 4 lbs)
- 1/4 cup olive oil
- 4 cloves garlic (minced)
- Zest of 2 lemons
- Juice of 2 lemons
- 2 teaspoons dried thyme
- Salt and black pepper to taste

Instructions:

1. Preheat the oven to 375°F (190°C).

2. Rinse the chicken inside and out, then pat dry with paper towels.

3. In a bowl, mix olive oil, minced garlic, lemon zest, lemon juice, dried thyme, salt, and black pepper.

4. Rub the chicken with the lemon-garlic mixture, ensuring it's evenly coated.

5. Tie the chicken legs together with kitchen twine.

6. Place the chicken on a rack in a roasting pan.

7. Roast in the preheated oven for approximately 1.5 to 2 hours, or until the internal temperature reaches 165°F (74°C).

8. Allow the chicken to rest for 15 minutes before carving.

Essential Nutritional Information:

- Calories: 400 per serving

- Fat: 25g

- Carbohydrates: 4g

- Protein: 25g

Tips:

- Baste the chicken with pan juices during roasting for extra flavor.

- Add root vegetables to the roasting pan for a complete meal.

Tricks:

- Tent the chicken with foil if it browns too quickly.

- Use a meat thermometer to ensure accurate cooking.

Ingredient Substitutions:

- Experiment with different herbs like rosemary or parsley.

- Substitute olive oil with melted butter for a richer flavor.

Creamy Mushroom Chicken

Summary: Delight in the velvety richness of Creamy Mushroom Chicken, a luscious dish that combines succulent chicken with a decadent mushroom and cream sauce. This recipe is a comforting and elegant choice for any occasion.

Protein Content: Approximately 30 grams of protein per serving.

Ingredients:

- 1.5 lbs boneless, skinless chicken breasts

- 2 tablespoons olive oil

- 1 lb cremini mushrooms (sliced)

- 4 cloves garlic (minced)

- 1 cup chicken broth

- 1 cup heavy cream

- 1 teaspoon dried thyme

- Salt and black pepper to taste

- Fresh parsley (chopped, for garnish)

Instructions:

1. In a large skillet, heat olive oil over medium-high heat.

2. Sear chicken breasts until browned on both sides. Remove from the skillet.

3. In the same skillet, add sliced mushrooms and minced garlic. Sauté until mushrooms release their moisture.

4. Pour in chicken broth, scraping the browned bits from the bottom of the skillet.

5. Reduce heat to medium, add heavy cream and dried thyme. Stir to combine.

6. Return seared chicken to the skillet, spooning the mushroom cream sauce over it.

7. Simmer for 15-20 minutes or until the chicken is cooked through.

8. Garnish with chopped fresh parsley before serving.

Essential Nutritional Information:

- Calories: 450 per serving

- Fat: 35g

- Carbohydrates: 6g

- Protein: 30g

Tips:

- Use a mix of wild mushrooms for added flavor complexity.

- Adjust the thickness of the sauce by adding more or less heavy cream.

Tricks:

- Deglaze the skillet with white wine for an extra layer of flavor.

- Add a touch of grated Parmesan to the sauce for a cheesy twist.

Ingredient Substitutions:

- Substitute heavy cream with half-and-half for a lighter option.

- Use bone-in, skin-on chicken thighs for a richer taste.

Honey Mustard Glazed Chicken

Summary: Indulge in the sweet and tangy goodness of Honey Mustard Glazed Chicken. This recipe features succulent chicken breasts glazed with a flavorful honey mustard sauce, creating a perfect harmony of taste in every bite.

Protein Content: Approximately 25 grams of protein per serving.

Ingredients:

- 1.5 lbs boneless, skinless chicken breasts

- 1/4 cup Dijon mustard

- 2 tablespoons honey

- 2 tablespoons olive oil

- 1 tablespoon soy sauce

- 2 cloves garlic (minced)

- Salt and black pepper to taste

- Fresh parsley (chopped, for garnish)

Instructions:

1. In a bowl, whisk together Dijon mustard, honey, olive oil, soy sauce, minced garlic, salt, and black pepper.

2. Place chicken breasts in a resealable plastic bag and pour the marinade over them. Seal the bag and refrigerate for at least 30 minutes.

3. Preheat the grill to medium-high heat.

4. Grill the chicken for 6-8 minutes per side or until fully cooked.

5. Let the chicken rest for a few minutes before slicing.

6. Garnish with chopped fresh parsley before serving.

Essential Nutritional Information:

- Calories: 350 per serving

- Fat: 15g

- Carbohydrates: 15g

- Protein: 25g

Tips:

- Brush additional marinade while grilling for extra flavor.

- Adjust honey and mustard ratios based on personal taste.

Tricks:

- Grill over cedar planks for a smoky flavor.

- Add a touch of lemon juice for a citrusy kick.

Ingredient Substitutions:

- Use whole-grain mustard for added texture.

- Substitute soy sauce with tamari or coconut aminos for a gluten-free option.

Chicken and Broccoli Stir Fry

Summary: Enjoy a quick and nutritious meal with Chicken and Broccoli Stir Fry. This dish features tender chicken and vibrant broccoli in a savory stir fry sauce, creating a perfect balance of flavors and textures.

Protein Content: Approximately 20 grams of protein per serving.

Ingredients:

- 1.5 lbs boneless, skinless chicken breasts (sliced)

- 4 cups broccoli florets

- 2 tablespoons soy sauce

- 1 tablespoon hoisin sauce

- 1 tablespoon rice vinegar

- 2 teaspoons Szechuan sauce

- 1 teaspoon sesame oil

- 2 tablespoons vegetable oil

- 2 cloves garlic (minced)

- 1 teaspoon ginger (grated)

- Red pepper flakes (optional, for extra heat)

- Green onions (sliced, for garnish)

- Sesame seeds (for garnish)

Instructions:

1. In a small bowl, mix soy sauce, hoisin sauce, rice vinegar, Szechuan sauce, and sesame oil to create the sauce.

2. Heat vegetable oil in a wok or large skillet over high heat.

3. Stir-fry sliced chicken until browned and cooked through. Remove from the pan.

4. In the same pan, add a bit more oil if needed. Stir-fry broccoli until crisp-tender.

5. Add minced garlic and grated ginger to the broccoli, sautéing for 1-2 minutes.

6. Return cooked chicken to the pan and pour the sauce over everything. Toss to coat.

7. If desired, sprinkle red pepper flakes for extra heat.

8. Garnish with sliced green onions and sesame seeds.

9. Serve over rice or noodles.

Essential Nutritional Information:

- Calories: 300 per serving

- Fat: 12g

- Carbohydrates: 15g

- Protein: 20g

Tips:

- Blanch broccoli before stir-frying for a vibrant color.

- Adjust Szechuan sauce quantity based on spice preference.

Tricks:

- Add a touch of honey for sweetness in the sauce.

- Use a high heat oil for a better stir-fry experience.

Ingredient Substitutions:

- Substitute chicken breasts with thigh meat.

- Replace broccoli with snap peas or bell peppers for variety.

Apple Cider Vinegar Chicken

Summary: Experience the tangy delight of Apple Cider Vinegar Chicken. This dish features marinated chicken in a flavorful blend of apple cider vinegar and spices, resulting in a zesty and delicious main course.

Protein Content: Approximately 25 grams of protein per serving.

Ingredients:

- 1.5 lbs bone-in, skin-on chicken thighs
- 1/2 cup apple cider vinegar
- 2 tablespoons olive oil
- 2 tablespoons honey
- 2 cloves garlic (minced)
- 1 teaspoon dried thyme
- 1 teaspoon smoked paprika
- Salt and black pepper to taste
- Fresh parsley (chopped, for garnish)

Instructions:

1. In a bowl, whisk together apple cider vinegar, olive oil, honey, minced garlic, dried thyme, smoked paprika, salt, and black pepper.

2. Place chicken thighs in a resealable plastic bag and pour the marinade over them. Seal the bag and refrigerate for at least 1 hour.

3. Preheat the oven to 400°F (200°C).

4. Place marinated chicken thighs on a baking sheet.

5. Bake for 35-40 minutes or until the chicken reaches an internal temperature of 165°F (74°C).

6. Garnish with chopped fresh parsley before serving.

Essential Nutritional Information:

- Calories: 380 per serving

- Fat: 25g

- Carbohydrates: 15g

- Protein: 25g

Tips:

- Reserve some marinade for drizzling after baking.

- Marinate chicken overnight for deeper flavor.

Tricks:

- Broil for the last 5 minutes for crispy skin.

- Use apple cider reduction for a sweeter glaze.

Ingredient Substitutions:

- Use boneless, skinless chicken thighs for a leaner option.

- Substitute honey with maple syrup for a different sweetness.

Mango Salsa Chicken

Summary: Elevate your chicken game with Mango Salsa Chicken, a vibrant dish that combines juicy chicken breasts with a refreshing mango salsa. This recipe is a burst of tropical flavors on your plate.

Protein Content: Approximately 30 grams of protein per serving.

Ingredients:

- 1.5 lbs boneless, skinless chicken breasts

- 2 ripe mangoes (peeled, pitted, and diced)

- 1 red bell pepper (diced)

- 1/2 red onion (finely chopped)

- 1 jalapeño (seeded and minced)

- Juice of 2 limes

- 1/4 cup fresh cilantro (chopped)

- Salt and black pepper to taste

- 2 tablespoons olive oil

Instructions:

1. In a bowl, combine diced mangoes, red bell pepper, red onion, jalapeño, lime juice, and chopped cilantro. Season with salt and black pepper. Set aside.

2. Season chicken breasts with salt and black pepper.

3. In a skillet, heat olive oil over medium-high heat.

4. Sear chicken breasts until golden brown on both sides and cooked through.

5. Serve chicken topped with mango salsa.

Essential Nutritional Information:

- Calories: 350 per serving

- Fat: 12g

- Carbohydrates: 30g

- Protein: 30g

Tips:

- Adjust jalapeño quantity for desired spice level.

- Let the mango salsa sit for a while for flavors to meld.

Tricks:

- Grill chicken for a smoky flavor.

- Add diced avocado to the salsa for creaminess.

Ingredient Substitutions:

- Substitute chicken breasts with chicken thighs.

- Use pineapple instead of mango for a different tropical twist.

Lemon Garlic Parmesan Chicken Wings

Summary: Savor the crispy goodness of Lemon Garlic Parmesan Chicken Wings. These wings are coated in a zesty lemon-garlic Parmesan mixture, delivering a burst of flavor in every crunchy bite.

Protein Content: Approximately 20 grams of protein per serving.

Ingredients:

- 2 lbs chicken wings

- 1/2 cup grated Parmesan cheese

- 1/4 cup fresh parsley (chopped)

- Zest of 2 lemons

- Juice of 2 lemons

- 4 cloves garlic (minced)

- 2 tablespoons olive oil

- Salt and black pepper to taste

Instructions:

1. Preheat the oven to 400°F (200°C).

2. In a bowl, combine grated Parmesan cheese, chopped fresh parsley, lemon zest, lemon juice, minced garlic, olive oil, salt, and black pepper.

3. Pat dry chicken wings with paper towels.

4. Toss chicken wings in the Parmesan mixture until well coated.

5. Place wings on a baking sheet lined with parchment paper.

6. Bake for 40-45 minutes or until wings are golden brown and crispy.

Essential Nutritional Information:

- Calories: 400 per serving

- Fat: 30g

- Carbohydrates: 5g

- Protein: 20g

Tips:

- Broil for the last 5 minutes for extra crispiness.

- Garnish with additional Parmesan before serving.

Tricks:

- Use a wire rack on the baking sheet for even crispiness.

- Drizzle with extra lemon juice before serving.

Ingredient Substitutions:

- Substitute grated Parmesan with Pecorino Romano for a sharper flavor.

- Use chicken drumettes instead of wings for variety.

Cajun Chicken Quinoa Bowl

Summary: Satisfy your taste buds with the Cajun Chicken Quinoa Bowl, a wholesome and protein-packed meal featuring seasoned chicken, quinoa, and a medley of colorful vegetables.

Protein Content: Approximately 30 grams of protein per serving.

Ingredients:

- 1.5 lbs boneless, skinless chicken thighs

- 1 cup quinoa

- 2 cups chicken broth

- 1 tablespoon Cajun seasoning

- 2 tablespoons olive oil

- 1 red bell pepper (sliced)

- 1 yellow bell pepper (sliced)

- 1 zucchini (sliced)

- 1 cup cherry tomatoes (halved)

- Fresh parsley (chopped, for garnish)

- Lemon wedges (for serving)

Instructions:

1. In a bowl, coat chicken thighs with Cajun seasoning.

2. Cook quinoa according to package instructions, using chicken broth for added flavor.

3. Heat olive oil in a skillet over medium-high heat.

4. Sear chicken thighs until browned and cooked through.

5. In the same skillet, sauté sliced bell peppers, zucchini, and cherry tomatoes until tender.

6. Slice cooked chicken thighs.

7. Assemble bowls with quinoa, sliced chicken, and sautéed vegetables.

8. Garnish with chopped fresh parsley and serve with lemon wedges.

Essential Nutritional Information:

- Calories: 450 per serving

- Fat: 15g

- Carbohydrates: 45g

- Protein: 30g

Tips:

- Customize veggies based on preference.

- Drizzle with olive oil and lemon before serving for extra freshness.

Tricks:

- Use pre-cooked rotisserie chicken for a quicker option.

- Roast vegetables for added depth of flavor.

Ingredient Substitutions:

- Substitute quinoa with brown rice or couscous.

- Use chicken breast instead of thighs for a leaner option.

Coconut Lime Chicken Skewers

Summary: Transport your taste buds to the tropics with Coconut Lime Chicken Skewers. This recipe features marinated chicken skewers infused with coconut and lime, creating a refreshing and flavorful dish.

Protein Content: Approximately 25 grams of protein per serving.

Ingredients:

- 1.5 lbs boneless, skinless chicken breasts (cut into chunks)

- 1 cup coconut milk

- Zest and juice of 2 limes

- 2 tablespoons soy sauce

- 2 tablespoons brown sugar

- 2 cloves garlic (minced)

- 1 teaspoon ground coriander

- 1 teaspoon ground cumin

- Salt and black pepper to taste

- Wooden skewers (soaked in water)

Instructions:

1. In a bowl, whisk together coconut milk, lime zest, lime juice, soy sauce, brown sugar, minced garlic, ground coriander, ground cumin, salt, and black pepper.

2. Thread chicken chunks onto soaked wooden skewers and place them in a shallow dish.

3. Pour the marinade over the chicken skewers, ensuring they are well coated. Marinate for at least 1 hour.

4. Preheat the grill to medium-high heat.

5. Grill the chicken skewers for 5-7 minutes per side or until fully cooked.

Essential Nutritional Information:

- Calories: 350 per serving

- Fat: 20g

- Carbohydrates: 10g

- Protein: 25g

Tips:

- Use full-fat coconut milk for richer flavor.

- Reserve some marinade for basting while grilling.

Tricks:

- Grill lime halves alongside chicken for extra charred lime flavor.

- Serve with a side of coconut rice for a complete meal.

Ingredient Substitutions:

- Substitute ground coriander with ground turmeric.

- Use chicken thighs for a juicier texture.

Spinach and Feta Stuffed Chicken Breast

Summary: Elevate your chicken dinner with Spinach and Feta Stuffed Chicken Breast. This recipe features succulent chicken breasts filled with a flavorful spinach and feta stuffing, creating a delicious and impressive dish.

Protein Content: Approximately 35 grams of protein per serving.

Ingredients:

- 1.5 lbs boneless, skinless chicken breasts

- 2 cups fresh spinach (chopped)

- 1/2 cup feta cheese (crumbled)

- 2 cloves garlic (minced)

- 1 tablespoon olive oil

- Salt and black pepper to taste

- Toothpicks or kitchen twine

Instructions:

1. Preheat the oven to 375°F (190°C).

2. In a skillet, sauté chopped spinach and minced garlic in olive oil until wilted.

3. Remove the skillet from heat and stir in crumbled feta.

4. Cut a pocket into each chicken breast.

5. Stuff each pocket with the spinach and feta mixture.

6. Secure the openings with toothpicks or tie with kitchen twine.

7. Season the outside of the chicken breasts with salt and black pepper.

8. Bake in the preheated oven for 25-30 minutes or until the chicken reaches an internal temperature of 165°F (74°C).

Essential Nutritional Information:

- Calories: 400 per serving

- Fat: 15g

- Carbohydrates: 2g

- Protein: 35g

Tips:

- Use toothpicks soaked in water to prevent burning.
- Customize the filling with sun-dried tomatoes or olives.

Tricks:

- Sear stuffed chicken breasts before baking for a golden crust.
- Drizzle with balsamic glaze before serving.

Ingredient Substitutions:

- Substitute feta with goat cheese or mozzarella.
- Use baby kale or arugula instead of spinach.

Pesto Grilled Chicken Salad

Summary: Embrace a light and flavorful meal with Pesto Grilled Chicken Salad. This recipe combines grilled chicken with vibrant greens and a basil pesto dressing, creating a refreshing and satisfying salad.

Protein Content: Approximately 25 grams of protein per serving.

Ingredients:

- 1.5 lbs boneless, skinless chicken breasts
- 8 cups mixed salad greens
- 1 cup cherry tomatoes (halved)
- 1 cucumber (sliced)
- 1/2 cup black olives (sliced)
- 1/4 cup pine nuts (toasted)
- Fresh basil leaves (for garnish)

Basil Pesto Dressing:

- 1 cup fresh basil leaves
- 1/2 cup grated Parmesan cheese

- 1/3 cup pine nuts

- 2 cloves garlic

- 1/2 cup extra virgin olive oil

- Salt and black pepper to taste

Instructions:

1. In a food processor, combine basil leaves, Parmesan cheese, pine nuts, and garlic for the dressing. Pulse until finely chopped.

2. With the processor running, slowly pour in the olive oil until a smooth pesto dressing forms. Season with salt and black pepper.

3. Season chicken breasts with salt and black pepper.

4. Preheat the grill to medium-high heat.

5. Grill the chicken for 6-8 minutes per side or until fully cooked.

6. In a large bowl, toss salad greens, cherry tomatoes, cucumber, and black olives.

7. Slice grilled chicken and place on top of the salad.

8. Drizzle pesto dressing over the salad and garnish with toasted pine nuts and fresh basil leaves.

Essential Nutritional Information:

- Calories: 400 per serving
- Fat: 30g
- Carbohydrates: 10g
- Protein: 25g

Tips:

- Marinate chicken in pesto for extra flavor.
- Toast pine nuts in a dry pan for a nuttier taste.

Tricks:

- Add avocado slices for creaminess.
- Serve with a side of crusty bread for a complete meal.

Ingredient Substitutions:

- Substitute pine nuts with walnuts.
- Use arugula or spinach for a peppery twist.

Teriyaki Chicken Lettuce Wraps

Summary: Experience the perfect blend of flavors in Teriyaki Chicken Lettuce Wraps. These wraps feature savory teriyaki chicken nestled in crisp lettuce leaves, creating a light and satisfying meal.

Protein Content: Approximately 20 grams of protein per serving.

Ingredients:

- 1.5 lbs boneless, skinless chicken thighs (cut into small pieces)

- 1/2 cup teriyaki sauce

- 1 tablespoon sesame oil

- 2 cloves garlic (minced)

- 1 teaspoon ginger (grated)

- 1 cup water chestnuts (drained and chopped)

- 1 cup shredded carrots

- 1/4 cup green onions (sliced)

- Butter lettuce leaves (for wrapping)

- Sesame seeds (for garnish)

Instructions:

1. In a bowl, marinate chicken pieces in teriyaki sauce, sesame oil, minced garlic, and grated ginger. Refrigerate for at least 30 minutes.

2. Heat a skillet over medium-high heat.

3. Cook marinated chicken until browned and fully cooked.

4. Add water chestnuts, shredded carrots, and sliced green onions to the skillet. Stir until well combined and heated through.

5. Spoon the teriyaki chicken mixture onto butter lettuce leaves.

6. Garnish with sesame seeds before serving.

Essential Nutritional Information:

- Calories: 300 per serving

- Fat: 15g

- Carbohydrates: 20g

- Protein: 20g

Tips:

- Use low-sodium teriyaki sauce for a healthier option.

- Add a squeeze of lime juice for brightness.

Tricks:

- Serve with a side of steamed rice for a heartier meal.

- Drizzle with extra teriyaki sauce before wrapping.

Ingredient Substitutions:

- Substitute chicken thighs with ground chicken.

- Use iceberg lettuce if butter lettuce is unavailable.

Greek Yogurt Chicken Salad

Summary: Enjoy a lighter take on chicken salad with the Greek Yogurt Chicken Salad. This recipe features tender chicken mixed with Greek yogurt, creating a protein-packed and flavorful dish.

Protein Content: Approximately 25 grams of protein per serving.

Ingredients:

- 1.5 lbs cooked chicken breasts (shredded)

- 1 cup Greek yogurt

- 1/2 cup cucumber (diced)

- 1/2 cup cherry tomatoes (halved)

- 1/4 cup red onion (finely chopped)

- 2 tablespoons fresh dill (chopped)

- 1 tablespoon lemon juice

- Salt and black pepper to taste

- Whole-grain bread or lettuce leaves (for serving)

Instructions:

1. In a bowl, combine shredded chicken, Greek yogurt, diced cucumber, halved cherry tomatoes, chopped red onion, fresh dill, and lemon juice.

2. Mix until all ingredients are well combined.

3. Season with salt and black pepper to taste.

4. Serve the Greek Yogurt Chicken Salad on whole-grain bread or lettuce leaves for a lighter option.

Essential Nutritional Information:

- Calories: 300 per serving

- Fat: 10g

- Carbohydrates: 10g

- Protein: 25g

Tips:

- Add a touch of garlic powder for extra flavor.

- Refrigerate for an hour before serving to let flavors meld.

Tricks:

- Use rotisserie chicken for a time-saving option.

- Mix in chopped Kalamata olives for a Mediterranean twist.

Ingredient Substitutions:

- Substitute Greek yogurt with plain yogurt.

- Add diced bell peppers for additional crunch.

Lemon Herb Grilled Chicken Thighs

Summary: Experience the vibrant flavors of Lemon Herb Grilled Chicken Thighs. This recipe features juicy chicken thighs marinated in a zesty lemon and herb mixture, grilled to perfection.

Protein Content: Approximately 30 grams of protein per serving.

Ingredients:

- 1.5 lbs bone-in, skin-on chicken thighs
- Zest and juice of 2 lemons
- 3 tablespoons olive oil
- 2 cloves garlic (minced)
- 1 tablespoon fresh rosemary (chopped)
- 1 tablespoon fresh thyme (chopped)
- Salt and black pepper to taste

Instructions:

1. In a bowl, whisk together lemon zest, lemon juice, olive oil, minced garlic, chopped rosemary, chopped thyme, salt, and black pepper.

2. Place chicken thighs in a resealable plastic bag and pour the marinade over them. Seal the bag and refrigerate for at least 2 hours or overnight.

3. Preheat the grill to medium-high heat.

4. Grill the chicken thighs for 15-20 minutes, turning occasionally, until fully cooked.

Essential Nutritional Information:

- Calories: 350 per serving

- Fat: 25g

- Carbohydrates: 2g

- Protein: 30g

Tips:

- Baste with marinade while grilling for added flavor.

- Let the chicken rest for a few minutes before serving.

Tricks:

- Grill over cedar planks for a smoky aroma.

- Finish with a squeeze of fresh lemon juice.

Ingredient Substitutions:

- Use boneless, skinless chicken thighs for a lighter option.

- Substitute rosemary and thyme with your favorite herbs.

Caprese Stuffed Balsamic Chicken

Summary: Elevate your chicken dinner with the Caprese Stuffed Balsamic Chicken. This recipe features succulent chicken breasts stuffed with mozzarella, tomatoes, and basil, drizzled with balsamic glaze.

Protein Content: Approximately 35 grams of protein per serving.

Ingredients:

- 1.5 lbs boneless, skinless chicken breasts

- 8 oz fresh mozzarella (sliced)

- 1 cup cherry tomatoes (sliced)

- Fresh basil leaves

- Balsamic glaze

- Salt and black pepper to taste

- Olive oil for drizzling

Instructions:

1. Preheat the oven to 375°F (190°C).

2. Cut a pocket into each chicken breast.

3. Stuff each pocket with slices of fresh mozzarella, cherry tomatoes, and fresh basil leaves.

4. Season the outside of the chicken breasts with salt and black pepper.

5. Place stuffed chicken breasts on a baking sheet.

6. Bake for 25-30 minutes or until the chicken reaches an internal temperature of 165°F (74°C).

7. Drizzle with balsamic glaze and olive oil before serving.

Essential Nutritional Information:

- Calories: 400 per serving

- Fat: 20g

- Carbohydrates: 5g

- Protein: 35g

Tips:

- Secure the pockets with toothpicks to prevent filling from falling out.

- Use heirloom tomatoes for a burst of color.

Tricks:

- Broil for the last 5 minutes for a golden finish.

- Garnish with additional fresh basil for a fragrant touch.

Ingredient Substitutions:

- Substitute mozzarella with goat cheese.

- Use a homemade balsamic reduction for drizzling.

Peanut Satay Chicken Skewers

Summary: Indulge in the rich and nutty flavors of Peanut Satay Chicken Skewers. This recipe features marinated chicken skewers grilled to perfection and served with a creamy peanut satay sauce.

Protein Content: Approximately 25 grams of protein per serving.

Ingredients:

- 1.5 lbs boneless, skinless chicken thighs (cut into strips)

- Wooden skewers (soaked in water)

- 1/2 cup peanut butter

- 1/4 cup soy sauce

- 2 tablespoons honey

- 1 tablespoon rice vinegar

- 2 cloves garlic (minced)

- 1 teaspoon ginger (grated)

- Crushed peanuts (for garnish)

- Fresh cilantro (chopped, for garnish)

Instructions:

1. In a bowl, whisk together peanut butter, soy sauce, honey, rice vinegar, minced garlic, and grated ginger to create the marinade.

2. Thread chicken strips onto soaked wooden skewers and place them in a shallow dish.

3. Pour the marinade over the chicken skewers, ensuring they are well coated. Marinate for at least 1 hour.

4. Preheat the grill to medium-high heat.

5. Grill the chicken skewers for 5-7 minutes per side or until fully cooked.

6. Garnish with crushed peanuts and chopped fresh cilantro.

Essential Nutritional Information:

- Calories: 380 per serving

- Fat: 25g

- Carbohydrates: 15g

- Protein: 25g

Tips:

- Add a splash of lime juice to the marinade for brightness.

- Reserve some peanut sauce for dipping.

Tricks:

- Use creamy or crunchy peanut butter based on preference.

- Skewer bell peppers and onions for added veggies.

Ingredient Substitutions:

- Substitute honey with maple syrup for a different sweetness.

- Use almond butter for a nutty variation.

Mediterranean Chicken Pita Pockets

Summary: Embark on a flavor journey with Mediterranean Chicken Pita Pockets. This recipe features seasoned chicken, crisp vegetables, and a zesty tzatziki sauce tucked into warm pita bread.

Protein Content: Approximately 30 grams of protein per serving.

Ingredients:

- 1.5 lbs boneless, skinless chicken breasts
- 4 whole-grain pita bread
- 1 cup cherry tomatoes (halved)
- 1 cucumber (diced)
- 1/2 red onion (sliced)
- 1/2 cup Kalamata olives (sliced)
- Feta cheese (crumbled)
- Fresh parsley (chopped, for garnish)

Tzatziki Sauce:

- 1 cup Greek yogurt

- 1 cucumber (grated and drained)

- 2 cloves garlic (minced)

- 1 tablespoon fresh dill (chopped)

- Salt and black pepper to taste

- Olive oil (for drizzling)

Instructions:

1. Season chicken breasts with salt and pepper.

2. Grill chicken until fully cooked, then slice into strips.

3. In a bowl, mix together Greek yogurt, grated and drained cucumber, minced garlic, chopped fresh dill, salt, and black pepper to create tzatziki sauce.

4. Warm pita bread.

5. Assemble pita pockets with grilled chicken, cherry tomatoes, diced cucumber, sliced red onion, Kalamata olives, and crumbled feta.

6. Drizzle tzatziki sauce over the filling and garnish with chopped fresh parsley.

Essential Nutritional Information:

- Calories: 450 per serving

- Fat: 15g

- Carbohydrates: 35g

- Protein: 30g

Tips:

- Toast pita bread for added crunch.

- Customize with hummus or roasted red peppers.

Tricks:

- Marinate chicken in Mediterranean spices for extra flavor.

- Use Greek-style pita for a thicker pocket.

Ingredient Substitutions:

- Substitute Greek yogurt with tzatziki-flavored yogurt.

- Use quinoa as a base for a grain bowl variation.

Sesame Ginger Chicken Stir-Fry

Summary: Delight your taste buds with the Sesame Ginger Chicken Stir-Fry. This recipe features tender chicken strips stir-fried with colorful vegetables in a flavorful sesame ginger sauce.

Protein Content: Approximately 25 grams of protein per serving.

Ingredients:

- 1.5 lbs boneless, skinless chicken breasts (sliced)

- 2 cups broccoli florets

- 1 bell pepper (sliced)

- 1 carrot (julienned)

- 2 tablespoons sesame oil

- 3 tablespoons soy sauce

- 1 tablespoon honey

- 1 tablespoon rice vinegar

- 1 tablespoon ginger (minced)

- 2 cloves garlic (minced)

- Sesame seeds (for garnish)

- Green onions (sliced, for garnish)

Instructions:

1. In a bowl, whisk together soy sauce, honey, rice vinegar, minced ginger, and minced garlic to create the sauce.

2. Heat sesame oil in a wok or large skillet over high heat.

3. Stir-fry chicken until browned and cooked through.

4. Add broccoli, bell pepper, and julienned carrot to the wok. Stir-fry until vegetables are tender-crisp.

5. Pour the sauce over the chicken and vegetables, tossing to coat evenly.

6. Garnish with sesame seeds and sliced green onions before serving.

Essential Nutritional Information:

- Calories: 350 per serving

- Fat: 15g

- Carbohydrates: 15g

- Protein: 25g

Tips:

- Partially freeze chicken for easier slicing.

- Use a variety of colorful bell peppers for visual appeal.

Tricks:

- Add a splash of lime juice for extra freshness.

- Serve over brown rice or cauliflower rice for a complete meal.

Ingredient Substitutions:

- Substitute honey with maple syrup for a different sweetness.

- Use tamari or coconut aminos for a gluten-free alternative.

Honey Mustard Glazed Chicken Skewers

Summary: Savor the sweet and tangy flavors of Honey Mustard Glazed Chicken Skewers. This recipe features marinated chicken skewers grilled to perfection and glazed with a luscious honey mustard sauce.

Protein Content: Approximately 20 grams of protein per serving.

Ingredients:

- 1.5 lbs boneless, skinless chicken thighs (cut into cubes)

- Wooden skewers (soaked in water)

- 1/4 cup Dijon mustard

- 2 tablespoons honey

- 1 tablespoon whole-grain mustard

- 1 tablespoon olive oil

- 1 clove garlic (minced)

- Salt and black pepper to taste

Instructions:

1. In a bowl, whisk together Dijon mustard, honey, whole-grain mustard, olive oil, minced garlic, salt, and black pepper to create the marinade.

2. Thread chicken cubes onto soaked wooden skewers and place them in a shallow dish.

3. Pour the marinade over the chicken skewers, ensuring they are well coated. Marinate for at least 1 hour.

4. Preheat the grill to medium-high heat.

5. Grill the chicken skewers for 5-7 minutes per side or until fully cooked.

6. Brush with additional honey mustard sauce before serving.

Essential Nutritional Information:

- Calories: 300 per serving

- Fat: 15g

- Carbohydrates: 15g

- Protein: 20g

Tips:

- Brush the grill with oil to prevent sticking.

- Reserve some sauce for dipping.

Tricks:

- Sprinkle with chopped fresh parsley for a burst of color.

- Grill lemon halves alongside for a citrusy touch.

Ingredient Substitutions:

- Use chicken breast instead of thighs for a leaner option.

- Substitute whole-grain mustard with spicy brown mustard.

Pesto Chicken Zoodle Bowl

Summary: Indulge in a low-carb delight with the Pesto Chicken Zoodle Bowl. This recipe features tender pesto-marinated chicken served over zucchini noodles, creating a flavorful and nutritious dish.

Protein Content: Approximately 30 grams of protein per serving.

Ingredients:

- 1.5 lbs boneless, skinless chicken breasts

- 4 medium zucchini (spiralized)

- 1 cup cherry tomatoes (halved)

- 1/2 cup basil pesto

- 2 tablespoons pine nuts (toasted)

- 1 tablespoon olive oil

- Salt and black pepper to taste

- Parmesan cheese (grated, for garnish)

Instructions:

1. Season chicken breasts with salt and black pepper.

2. In a bowl, coat chicken with basil pesto. Marinate for at least 30 minutes.

3. Heat olive oil in a skillet over medium-high heat.

4. Cook chicken until browned and fully cooked.

5. Spiralize zucchini into noodles and sauté briefly in the skillet until just tender.

6. Assemble bowls with zucchini noodles, sliced pesto chicken, and halved cherry tomatoes.

7. Garnish with toasted pine nuts and grated Parmesan cheese.

Essential Nutritional Information:

- Calories: 400 per serving

- Fat: 25g

- Carbohydrates: 10g

- Protein: 30g

Tips:

- Use a variety of colored cherry tomatoes for visual appeal.

- Drizzle with extra pesto before serving.

Tricks:

- Add a squeeze of lemon juice for brightness.

- Substitute pine nuts with sliced almonds.

Ingredient Substitutions:

- Use store-bought or homemade pesto.

- Replace zucchini noodles with spaghetti squash for variety.

Lime Chili Grilled Chicken Tacos

Summary: Bring a burst of flavor to your table with Lime Chili Grilled Chicken Tacos. This recipe features marinated chicken grilled to perfection and served in warm tortillas with vibrant toppings.

Protein Content: Approximately 25 grams of protein per serving.

Ingredients:

- 1.5 lbs boneless, skinless chicken thighs
- Corn or flour tortillas
- 2 limes (zested and juiced)
- 2 tablespoons olive oil
- 1 tablespoon chili powder
- 1 teaspoon cumin
- 1 teaspoon garlic powder
- 1 teaspoon onion powder
- Salt and black pepper to taste
- Fresh cilantro (chopped, for garnish)

- Salsa, avocado, and lime wedges (for serving)

Instructions:

1. In a bowl, whisk together lime zest, lime juice, olive oil, chili powder, cumin, garlic powder, onion powder, salt, and black pepper to create the marinade.

2. Coat chicken thighs with the marinade. Marinate for at least 30 minutes.

3. Preheat the grill to medium-high heat.

4. Grill chicken thighs for 5-7 minutes per side or until fully cooked.

5. Slice grilled chicken into strips.

6. Warm tortillas on the grill or in a dry skillet.

7. Assemble tacos with chicken strips, fresh cilantro, salsa, sliced avocado, and a squeeze of lime juice.

Essential Nutritional Information:

- Calories: 350 per serving

- Fat: 15g

- Carbohydrates: 20g

- Protein: 25g

Tips:

- Double up on tortillas for extra stability.

- Char tortillas for added smokiness.

Tricks:

- Marinate chicken in a sealed plastic bag for easy cleanup.

- Grill sliced jalapeños for a spicy kick.

Ingredient Substitutions:

- Substitute chicken thighs with chicken breast.

- Use your favorite salsa or pico de gallo.

Coconut Curry Chicken Skewers

Summary: Take your taste buds on a journey with Coconut Curry Chicken Skewers. This recipe features marinated chicken skewers infused with coconut milk and curry flavors, grilled to perfection.

Protein Content: Approximately 30 grams of protein per serving.

Ingredients:

- 1.5 lbs boneless, skinless chicken breasts (cut into chunks)

- Wooden skewers (soaked in water)

- 1 cup coconut milk

- 2 tablespoons red curry paste

- 1 tablespoon soy sauce

- 1 tablespoon brown sugar

- 1 tablespoon lime juice

- 2 cloves garlic (minced)

- Fresh cilantro (chopped, for garnish)

- Crushed peanuts (for garnish)

Instructions:

1. In a bowl, whisk together coconut milk, red curry paste, soy sauce, brown sugar, lime juice, and minced garlic to create the marinade.

2. Thread chicken chunks onto soaked wooden skewers and place them in a shallow dish.

3. Pour the marinade over the chicken skewers, ensuring they are well coated. Marinate for at least 1 hour.

4. Preheat the grill to medium-high heat.

5. Grill the chicken skewers for 5-7 minutes per side or until fully cooked.

6. Garnish with chopped fresh cilantro and crushed peanuts before serving.

Essential Nutritional Information:

- Calories: 400 per serving

- Fat: 20g

- Carbohydrates: 10g

- Protein: 30g

Tips:

- Use full-fat coconut milk for richer flavor.

- Serve with a side of jasmine rice or quinoa.

Tricks:

- Skewer bell peppers and onions for added color.

- Brush with extra marinade while grilling.

Ingredient Substitutions:

- Substitute red curry paste with yellow or green curry paste.

- Use almond butter for a nuttier taste in the marinade.

Mango Habanero Grilled Chicken

Summary: Spice up your grilling game with Mango Habanero Grilled Chicken. This recipe features succulent chicken marinated in a sweet and spicy mango habanero sauce, creating a flavor-packed dish.

Protein Content: Approximately 25 grams of protein per serving.

Ingredients:

- 1.5 lbs boneless, skinless chicken thighs

- 1 cup mango (diced)

- 2 habanero peppers (seeded and minced)

- 1/4 cup lime juice

- 2 tablespoons honey

- 2 tablespoons soy sauce

- 2 cloves garlic (minced)

- Salt and black pepper to taste

- Fresh cilantro (chopped, for garnish)

Instructions:

1. In a blender, combine diced mango, minced habanero peppers, lime juice, honey, soy sauce, minced garlic, salt, and black pepper. Blend until smooth.

2. Place chicken thighs in a resealable plastic bag and pour the mango habanero sauce over them. Seal the bag and marinate for at least 2 hours.

3. Preheat the grill to medium-high heat.

4. Grill chicken thighs for 5-7 minutes per side or until fully cooked.

5. Garnish with chopped fresh cilantro before serving.

Essential Nutritional Information:

- Calories: 300 per serving

- Fat: 15g

- Carbohydrates: 15g

- Protein: 25g

Tips:

- Adjust habanero quantity for preferred spice level.

- Reserve some marinade for basting.

Tricks:

- Grill slices of mango for a fruity side.

- Serve with a cooling cucumber salad.

Ingredient Substitutions:

- Substitute habanero with jalapeño for milder heat.

- Use agave syrup instead of honey.

Cajun Lime Grilled Chicken

Summary: Infuse bold flavors into your dinner with Cajun Lime Grilled Chicken. This recipe features Cajun-spiced chicken grilled to perfection with a zesty lime kick.

Protein Content: Approximately 30 grams of protein per serving.

Ingredients:

- 1.5 lbs boneless, skinless chicken breasts

- 2 tablespoons Cajun seasoning

- Zest and juice of 2 limes

- 2 tablespoons olive oil

- 2 cloves garlic (minced)

- Salt and black pepper to taste

- Fresh parsley (chopped, for garnish)

Instructions:

1. In a bowl, mix Cajun seasoning, lime zest, lime juice, olive oil, minced garlic, salt, and black pepper.

2. Coat chicken breasts with the Cajun lime mixture. Marinate for at least 30 minutes.

3. Preheat the grill to medium-high heat.

4. Grill chicken breasts for 6-8 minutes per side or until fully cooked.

5. Garnish with chopped fresh parsley before serving.

Essential Nutritional Information:

- Calories: 320 per serving

- Fat: 15g

- Carbohydrates: 2g

- Protein: 30g

Tips:

- Adjust Cajun seasoning to suit your spice preference.

- Squeeze extra lime juice before serving.

Tricks:

- Grill lime halves alongside chicken for added flavor.

- Serve with a side of seasoned roasted vegetables.

Ingredient Substitutions:

- Use blackened seasoning as a Cajun alternative.

- Replace olive oil with melted butter.

Almond Crusted Baked Chicken

Summary: Add a crunchy twist to your chicken with Almond Crusted Baked Chicken. This recipe features chicken breasts coated in a flavorful almond crust, baked to golden perfection.

Protein Content: Approximately 35 grams of protein per serving.

Ingredients:

- 1.5 lbs boneless, skinless chicken breasts

- 1 cup almonds (finely ground)

- 1/2 cup grated Parmesan cheese

- 1 teaspoon garlic powder

- 1 teaspoon onion powder

- 1 teaspoon dried oregano

- Salt and black pepper to taste

- 2 eggs (beaten)

Instructions:

1. Preheat the oven to 400°F (200°C). Line a baking sheet with parchment paper.

2. In a bowl, mix ground almonds, grated Parmesan, garlic powder, onion powder, dried oregano, salt, and black pepper.

3. Dip each chicken breast into beaten eggs, then coat with the almond mixture.

4. Place the coated chicken breasts on the prepared baking sheet.

5. Bake for 20-25 minutes or until the chicken reaches an internal temperature of 165°F (74°C).

Essential Nutritional Information:

- Calories: 400 per serving

- Fat: 25g

- Carbohydrates: 5g

- Protein: 35g

Tips:

- Use a food processor to finely grind almonds.

- Add a pinch of cayenne for a spicy kick.

Tricks:

- Spray chicken with cooking spray for extra crispiness.

- Serve with a side of lemon wedges.

Ingredient Substitutions:

- Substitute almonds with pecans or walnuts.

- Use nutritional yeast instead of Parmesan for a dairy-free option.

Miso Glazed Chicken Skewers

Summary: Elevate your grilling experience with Miso Glazed Chicken Skewers. This recipe features chicken skewers marinated in a savory miso glaze, delivering a perfect umami flavor.

Protein Content: Approximately 25 grams of protein per serving.

Ingredients:

- 1.5 lbs boneless, skinless chicken thighs (cut into strips)

- Wooden skewers (soaked in water)

- 1/4 cup miso paste

- 2 tablespoons soy sauce

- 2 tablespoons mirin

- 1 tablespoon honey

- 1 teaspoon sesame oil

- 2 cloves garlic (minced)

- Sesame seeds (for garnish)

- Green onions (sliced, for garnish)

Instructions:

1. In a bowl, whisk together miso paste, soy sauce, mirin, honey, sesame oil, and minced garlic to create the glaze.

2. Thread chicken strips onto soaked wooden skewers and place them in a shallow dish.

3. Pour the miso glaze over the chicken skewers, ensuring they are well coated. Marinate for at least 1 hour.

4. Preheat the grill to medium-high heat.

5. Grill the chicken skewers for 5-7 minutes per side or until fully cooked.

6. Garnish with sesame seeds and sliced green onions before serving.

Essential Nutritional Information:

- Calories: 320 per serving

- Fat: 15g

- Carbohydrates: 10g

- Protein: 25g

Tips:

- Adjust honey for preferred sweetness.

- Baste with extra miso glaze while grilling.

Tricks:

- Grill pineapple chunks alongside for a tropical touch.

- Serve over a bed of jasmine rice.

Ingredient Substitutions:

- Substitute mirin with rice vinegar and a pinch of sugar.

- Use white miso paste for a milder flavor.

Sun-Dried Tomato Pesto Chicken

Summary: Experience the rich flavors of Sun-Dried Tomato Pesto Chicken. This recipe features chicken breasts smothered in a sun-dried tomato pesto, creating a delicious and comforting dish.

Protein Content: Approximately 30 grams of protein per serving.

Ingredients:

- 1.5 lbs boneless, skinless chicken breasts
- 1/2 cup sun-dried tomatoes (packed in oil)
- 1/4 cup pine nuts (toasted)
- 2 cloves garlic
- 1/2 cup fresh basil leaves
- 1/2 cup grated Parmesan cheese
- 1/4 cup olive oil
- Salt and black pepper to taste

Instructions:

1. Preheat the oven to 375°F (190°C).

2. In a food processor, combine sun-dried tomatoes, toasted pine nuts, garlic, fresh basil, grated Parmesan, olive oil, salt, and black pepper. Blend until a pesto consistency is reached.

3. Season chicken breasts with salt and black pepper.

4. Spread a generous layer of sun-dried tomato pesto over each chicken breast.

5. Place the chicken breasts on a baking sheet.

6. Bake for 25-30 minutes or until the chicken reaches an internal temperature of 165°F (74°C).

Essential Nutritional Information:

- Calories: 400 per serving

- Fat: 25g

- Carbohydrates: 5g

- Protein: 30g

Tips:

- Use oil-packed sun-dried tomatoes for richer flavor.

- Reserve some pesto for drizzling.

Tricks:

- Top with fresh cherry tomatoes for a burst of freshness.

- Serve over a bed of quinoa or couscous.

Ingredient Substitutions:

- Substitute pine nuts with almonds or walnuts.

- Use a mix of sun-dried and cherry tomatoes for a varied texture.

Teriyaki Pineapple Chicken Skewers

Summary: Delight your taste buds with Teriyaki Pineapple Chicken Skewers. This recipe features marinated chicken skewers with sweet and tangy teriyaki sauce, grilled to perfection with juicy pineapple chunks.

Protein Content: Approximately 25 grams of protein per serving.

Ingredients:

- 1.5 lbs boneless, skinless chicken thighs (cut into chunks)

- Wooden skewers (soaked in water)

- 1 cup pineapple juice

- 1/4 cup soy sauce

- 2 tablespoons honey

- 1 tablespoon rice vinegar

- 1 teaspoon ginger (minced)

- 2 cloves garlic (minced)

- Pineapple chunks (for skewering)

Instructions:

1. In a bowl, whisk together pineapple juice, soy sauce, honey, rice vinegar, minced ginger, and minced garlic to create the teriyaki marinade.

2. Thread chicken chunks and pineapple onto soaked wooden skewers and place them in a shallow dish.

3. Pour the teriyaki marinade over the chicken skewers, ensuring they are well coated. Marinate for at least 1 hour.

4. Preheat the grill to medium-high heat.

5. Grill the chicken skewers for 5-7 minutes per side or until fully cooked.

6. Baste with extra teriyaki sauce while grilling.

Essential Nutritional Information:

- Calories: 300 per serving

- Fat: 15g

- Carbohydrates: 20g

- Protein: 25g

Tips:

- Reserve some marinade for dipping.

- Grill until pineapple caramelizes for extra sweetness.

Tricks:

- Use metal skewers for quicker cooking.

- Garnish with sesame seeds and green onions.

Ingredient Substitutions:

- Substitute pineapple juice with orange juice.

- Use tamari or coconut aminos for a gluten-free alternative.

Chimichurri Grilled Chicken

Summary: Elevate your grilling game with Chimichurri Grilled Chicken. This recipe features succulent chicken breasts marinated in a vibrant chimichurri sauce, delivering a burst of fresh and herby flavors.

Protein Content: Approximately 30 grams of protein per serving.

Ingredients:

- 1.5 lbs boneless, skinless chicken breasts
- 1 cup fresh parsley (chopped)
- 1/2 cup fresh cilantro (chopped)
- 3 cloves garlic (minced)
- 1/4 cup red wine vinegar
- 1/2 cup olive oil
- 1 teaspoon dried oregano
- Salt and black pepper to taste
- Red pepper flakes (optional, for heat)

Instructions:

1. In a food processor, combine fresh parsley, fresh cilantro, minced garlic, red wine vinegar, olive oil, dried oregano, salt, black pepper, and red pepper flakes (if using). Pulse until a coarse chimichurri sauce is formed.

2. Season chicken breasts with salt and black pepper.

3. Coat chicken breasts with chimichurri sauce. Marinate for at least 30 minutes.

4. Preheat the grill to medium-high heat.

5. Grill chicken breasts for 6-8 minutes per side or until fully cooked.

6. Drizzle with extra chimichurri sauce before serving.

Essential Nutritional Information:

- Calories: 350 per serving

- Fat: 25g

- Carbohydrates: 2g

- Protein: 30g

Tips:

- Adjust red pepper flakes for preferred spice.

- Let chicken rest before slicing.

Tricks:

- Reserve some chimichurri for serving.

- Serve over a bed of quinoa or couscous.

Ingredient Substitutions:

- Substitute red wine vinegar with white wine vinegar.

- Use a mix of parsley and basil for a different herb profile.

Lemon Garlic Herb Grilled Chicken

Summary: Enjoy the classic combination of Lemon Garlic Herb Grilled Chicken. This recipe features chicken thighs marinated in a zesty lemon garlic herb mixture, delivering a perfect balance of flavors.

Protein Content: Approximately 25 grams of protein per serving.

Ingredients:

- 1.5 lbs boneless, skinless chicken thighs

- Zest and juice of 2 lemons

- 4 cloves garlic (minced)

- 1/4 cup fresh rosemary (chopped)

- 1/4 cup fresh thyme leaves

- 1/2 cup olive oil

- Salt and black pepper to taste

Instructions:

1. In a bowl, mix lemon zest, lemon juice, minced garlic, chopped fresh rosemary, chopped fresh thyme, olive oil, salt, and black pepper.

2. Coat chicken thighs with the lemon garlic herb mixture. Marinate for at least 30 minutes.

3. Preheat the grill to medium-high heat.

4. Grill chicken thighs for 5-7 minutes per side or until fully cooked.

5. Garnish with extra fresh herbs before serving.

Essential Nutritional Information:

- Calories: 320 per serving

- Fat: 20g

- Carbohydrates: 2g

- Protein: 25g

Tips:

- Grill lemon halves for a finishing touch.

- Use a meat thermometer to ensure proper doneness.

Tricks:

- Serve with a side of grilled vegetables.

- Drizzle with a bit of extra virgin olive oil.

Ingredient Substitutions:

- Substitute rosemary and thyme with basil and oregano.

- Use Meyer lemons for a sweeter citrus flavor.

Balsamic Glazed Caprese Chicken

Summary: Indulge in the exquisite flavors of Balsamic Glazed Caprese Chicken. This recipe features grilled chicken breasts topped with fresh mozzarella, tomatoes, and basil, drizzled with a balsamic glaze.

Protein Content: Approximately 30 grams of protein per serving.

Ingredients:

- 1.5 lbs boneless, skinless chicken breasts
- 1 cup fresh mozzarella balls (sliced)
- 1 cup cherry tomatoes (halved)
- Fresh basil leaves
- 1/2 cup balsamic glaze
- Salt and black pepper to taste

Instructions:

1. Season chicken breasts with salt and black pepper.
2. Preheat the grill to medium-high heat.

3. Grill chicken breasts for 6-8 minutes per side or until fully cooked.

4. During the last minute of grilling, top each chicken breast with sliced fresh mozzarella.

5. Remove chicken from the grill and let it rest for a few minutes.

6. Plate the chicken and top with cherry tomatoes and fresh basil.

7. Drizzle with balsamic glaze before serving.

Essential Nutritional Information:

- Calories: 350 per serving

- Fat: 15g

- Carbohydrates: 10g

- Protein: 30g

Tips:

- Use heirloom tomatoes for a colorful twist.

- Garnish with a sprinkle of flaky sea salt.

Tricks:

- Grill slices of baguette for a complete Caprese experience.

- Drizzle with extra virgin olive oil.

Ingredient Substitutions:

- Make your own balsamic glaze by reducing balsamic vinegar.

- Substitute fresh mozzarella with burrata for added creaminess.

Asian Peanut Chicken Lettuce Wraps

Summary: Enjoy a light and flavorful meal with Asian Peanut Chicken Lettuce Wraps. This recipe features ground chicken cooked in a savory peanut sauce, served in crisp lettuce cups.

Protein Content: Approximately 20 grams of protein per serving.

Ingredients:

- 1.5 lbs ground chicken

- 1/2 cup hoisin sauce

- 1/4 cup soy sauce

- 2 tablespoons peanut butter

- 1 tablespoon sesame oil

- 2 cloves garlic (minced)

- 1 teaspoon ginger (minced)

- 1/4 cup green onions (sliced)

- 1/4 cup peanuts (chopped, for garnish)

- Butter lettuce leaves (for serving)

Instructions:

1. In a bowl, whisk together hoisin sauce, soy sauce, peanut butter, sesame oil, minced garlic, and minced ginger to create the peanut sauce.

2. In a skillet over medium heat, cook ground chicken until fully cooked.

3. Pour the peanut sauce over the cooked chicken, stirring to coat evenly. Cook for an additional 2-3 minutes.

4. Stir in sliced green onions.

5. Spoon the peanut chicken mixture into butter lettuce leaves.

6. Garnish with chopped peanuts before serving.

Essential Nutritional Information:

- Calories: 300 per serving

- Fat: 15g

- Carbohydrates: 10g

- Protein: 20g

Tips:

- Add a squeeze of lime juice for brightness.

- Serve with a side of steamed rice or quinoa.

Tricks:

- Garnish with cilantro for added freshness.

- Use crunchy peanut butter for extra texture.

Ingredient Substitutions:

- Substitute hoisin sauce with sweet chili sauce.

- Use ground turkey or tofu as a chicken alternative.

Lemon Herb Grilled Chicken Thighs

Summary: Savor the bright and savory flavors of Lemon Herb Grilled Chicken Thighs. This recipe features succulent chicken thighs marinated in a zesty lemon herb mixture, grilled to perfection.

Protein Content: Approximately 25 grams of protein per serving.

Ingredients:

- 1.5 lbs boneless, skinless chicken thighs
- Zest and juice of 2 lemons
- 4 cloves garlic (minced)
- 1/4 cup fresh parsley (chopped)
- 1/4 cup fresh thyme leaves
- 1/2 cup olive oil
- Salt and black pepper to taste

Instructions:

1. In a bowl, mix lemon zest, lemon juice, minced garlic, chopped fresh parsley, chopped fresh thyme, olive oil, salt, and black pepper.

2. Coat chicken thighs with the lemon herb mixture. Marinate for at least 30 minutes.

3. Preheat the grill to medium-high heat.

4. Grill chicken thighs for 5-7 minutes per side or until fully cooked.

5. Garnish with extra fresh herbs before serving.

Essential Nutritional Information:

- Calories: 320 per serving

- Fat: 20g

- Carbohydrates: 2g

- Protein: 25g

Tips:

- Grill lemon halves for a finishing touch.

- Use a meat thermometer to ensure proper doneness.

Tricks:

- Serve with a side of grilled vegetables.

- Drizzle with a bit of extra virgin olive oil.

Ingredient Substitutions:

- Substitute thyme with rosemary or oregano.

- Use Meyer lemons for a sweeter citrus flavor.

Pesto Stuffed Grilled Chicken Breasts

Summary: Elevate your grilling experience with Pesto Stuffed Grilled Chicken Breasts. This recipe features chicken breasts stuffed with flavorful pesto and grilled to juicy perfection.

Protein Content: Approximately 30 grams of protein per serving.

Ingredients:

- 1.5 lbs boneless, skinless chicken breasts

- 1/2 cup pesto sauce

- 1 cup cherry tomatoes (halved)

- 1/2 cup mozzarella cheese (shredded)

- Salt and black pepper to taste

- Olive oil for brushing

Instructions:

1. Preheat the grill to medium-high heat.

2. Butterfly each chicken breast by slicing horizontally, leaving one edge intact.

3. Spread a layer of pesto inside each butterflied chicken breast.

4. Place halved cherry tomatoes on one side and sprinkle shredded mozzarella on top.

5. Fold the chicken breast over the filling, creating a stuffed pocket. Secure with toothpicks if needed.

6. Brush each stuffed chicken breast with olive oil.

7. Grill for 6-8 minutes per side or until the chicken is cooked through.

Essential Nutritional Information:

- Calories: 350 per serving

- Fat: 15g

- Carbohydrates: 5g

- Protein: 30g

Tips:

- Use a variety of pesto flavors.

- Let chicken rest before slicing.

Tricks:

- Grill until cheese is melted and bubbly.

- Serve with a side of mixed greens.

Ingredient Substitutions:

- Substitute mozzarella with feta or goat cheese.

- Use sun-dried tomato pesto for added richness.

Soy Ginger Glazed Chicken Skewers

Summary: Experience the delightful blend of flavors in Soy Ginger Glazed Chicken Skewers. This recipe features marinated chicken skewers with a sweet and savory soy ginger glaze, grilled to perfection.

Protein Content: Approximately 25 grams of protein per serving.

Ingredients:

- 1.5 lbs boneless, skinless chicken thighs (cut into strips)

- Wooden skewers (soaked in water)

- 1/4 cup soy sauce

- 2 tablespoons honey

- 1 tablespoon sesame oil

- 2 cloves garlic (minced)

- 1 teaspoon ginger (minced)

- Sesame seeds (for garnish)

- Green onions (sliced, for garnish)

Instructions:

1. In a bowl, whisk together soy sauce, honey, sesame oil, minced garlic, and minced ginger to create the marinade.

2. Thread chicken strips onto soaked wooden skewers and place them in a shallow dish.

3. Pour the soy ginger marinade over the chicken skewers, ensuring they are well coated. Marinate for at least 1 hour.

4. Preheat the grill to medium-high heat.

5. Grill the chicken skewers for 5-7 minutes per side or until fully cooked.

6. Garnish with sesame seeds and sliced green onions before serving.

Essential Nutritional Information:

- Calories: 320 per serving

- Fat: 15g

- Carbohydrates: 10g

- Protein: 25g

Tips:

- Baste with extra marinade while grilling.

- Serve over a bed of jasmine rice.

Tricks:

- Grill pineapple chunks alongside for a tropical touch.

- Use tamari for a gluten-free alternative.

Ingredient Substitutions:

- Substitute honey with maple syrup.

- Use ground ginger if fresh is not available.

Mediterranean Grilled Chicken Salad

Summary: Enjoy a refreshing and nutritious meal with Mediterranean Grilled Chicken Salad. This recipe features grilled chicken breasts served over a bed of crisp greens, cherry tomatoes, cucumber, feta cheese, and olives.

Protein Content: Approximately 25 grams of protein per serving.

Ingredients:

- 1.5 lbs boneless, skinless chicken breasts

- Mixed salad greens

- Cherry tomatoes (halved)

- Cucumber (sliced)

- Feta cheese (crumbled)

- Kalamata olives (pitted)

- Olive oil for dressing

- Lemon juice for dressing

- Dried oregano for dressing

- Salt and black pepper to taste

Instructions:

1. Season chicken breasts with salt and black pepper.

2. Preheat the grill to medium-high heat.

3. Grill chicken breasts for 6-8 minutes per side or until fully cooked.

4. In a large bowl, arrange mixed salad greens, cherry tomatoes, cucumber slices, crumbled feta, and Kalamata olives.

5. Slice grilled chicken and place it on top of the salad.

6. In a small bowl, whisk together olive oil, lemon juice, dried oregano, salt, and black pepper to create the dressing.

7. Drizzle the dressing over the salad before serving.

Essential Nutritional Information:

- Calories: 350 per serving

- Fat: 15g

- Carbohydrates: 10g

- Protein: 25g

Tips:

- Grill red onions for added flavor.

- Toss salad with dressing just before serving.

Tricks:

- Grill lemon halves for a burst of citrus.

- Use a variety of salad greens for complexity.

Ingredient Substitutions:

- Substitute feta with goat cheese.

- Use balsamic vinaigrette as an alternative dressing.

Coconut Lime Grilled Chicken Skewers

Summary: Transport your taste buds to the tropics with Coconut Lime Grilled Chicken Skewers. This recipe features marinated chicken skewers infused with coconut and lime flavors, grilled to perfection.

Protein Content: Approximately 20 grams of protein per serving.

Ingredients:

- 1.5 lbs boneless, skinless chicken thighs (cut into strips)

- Wooden skewers (soaked in water)

- 1/2 cup coconut milk

- Zest and juice of 2 limes

- 2 tablespoons soy sauce

- 1 tablespoon honey

- 1 teaspoon ginger (minced)

- 2 cloves garlic (minced)

- Fresh cilantro (chopped, for garnish)

Instructions:

1. In a bowl, whisk together coconut milk, lime zest, lime juice, soy sauce, honey, minced ginger, and minced garlic to create the marinade.

2. Thread chicken strips onto soaked wooden skewers and place them in a shallow dish.

3. Pour the coconut lime marinade over the chicken skewers, ensuring they are well coated. Marinate for at least 1 hour.

4. Preheat the grill to medium-high heat.

5. Grill the chicken skewers for 5-7 minutes per side or until fully cooked.

6. Garnish with chopped fresh cilantro before serving.

Essential Nutritional Information:

- Calories: 300 per serving

- Fat: 15g

- Carbohydrates: 10g

- Protein: 20g

Tips:

- Reserve some marinade for dipping.

- Serve over a bed of coconut rice.

Tricks:

- Grill pineapple chunks alongside for a tropical touch.

- Use coconut aminos for a gluten-free alternative.

Ingredient Substitutions:

- Substitute honey with agave syrup.

- Use lemongrass for an extra citrusy kick.

Mango Habanero Grilled Chicken

Summary: Embark on a flavor journey with Mango Habanero Grilled Chicken. This recipe features chicken thighs marinated in a tropical blend of mango and spicy habanero, grilled to perfection.

Protein Content: Approximately 25 grams of protein per serving.

Ingredients:

- 1.5 lbs boneless, skinless chicken thighs

- 1 cup mango (diced)

- 1 habanero pepper (seeded and minced)

- 2 tablespoons lime juice

- 2 tablespoons olive oil

- 2 cloves garlic (minced)

- Salt and black pepper to taste

Instructions:

1. In a blender, combine diced mango, minced habanero pepper, lime juice, olive oil, minced garlic, salt, and black pepper. Blend until smooth.

2. Season chicken thighs with salt and black pepper.

3. Coat chicken thighs with the mango habanero marinade. Marinate for at least 30 minutes.

4. Preheat the grill to medium-high heat.

5. Grill chicken thighs for 5-7 minutes per side or until fully cooked.

6. Garnish with extra diced mango before serving.

Essential Nutritional Information:

- Calories: 320 per serving

- Fat: 20g

- Carbohydrates: 10g

- Protein: 25g

Tips:

- Adjust habanero quantity for desired spice level.

- Grill lime halves for a citrusy touch.

Tricks:

- Serve with a side of coconut rice.

- Drizzle with extra marinade before serving.

Ingredient Substitutions:

- Substitute habanero with jalapeño for milder heat.

- Use peach or pineapple as a mango alternative.

Cajun Spiced Grilled Chicken

Summary: Spice up your grilling game with Cajun Spiced Grilled Chicken. This recipe features chicken breasts seasoned with a bold blend of Cajun spices, delivering a flavorful and satisfying dish.

Protein Content: Approximately 30 grams of protein per serving.

Ingredients:

- 1.5 lbs boneless, skinless chicken breasts

- 2 tablespoons Cajun seasoning

- 1 tablespoon olive oil

- 1 teaspoon paprika

- 1 teaspoon garlic powder

- 1 teaspoon onion powder

- 1/2 teaspoon thyme

- Salt and black pepper to taste

Instructions:

1. In a bowl, mix Cajun seasoning, olive oil, paprika, garlic powder, onion powder, thyme, salt, and black pepper to create the spice rub.

2. Season chicken breasts with the Cajun spice rub, ensuring even coverage.

3. Preheat the grill to medium-high heat.

4. Grill chicken breasts for 6-8 minutes per side or until fully cooked.

5. Allow chicken to rest before slicing.

Essential Nutritional Information:

- Calories: 350 per serving

- Fat: 15g

- Carbohydrates: 2g

- Protein: 30g

Tips:

- Adjust Cajun seasoning for preferred spice intensity.

- Serve with a side of creamy coleslaw.

Tricks:

- Add a squeeze of lemon juice before serving.

- Grill corn on the cob as a side dish.

Ingredient Substitutions:

- Create a homemade Cajun seasoning mix.

- Use bone-in, skin-on chicken for extra juiciness.

Harissa Yogurt Marinated Chicken

Summary: Experience the bold and tangy flavors of Harissa Yogurt Marinated Chicken. This recipe features chicken thighs marinated in a zesty blend of harissa and yogurt, creating a succulent and flavorful dish.

Protein Content: Approximately 25 grams of protein per serving.

Ingredients:

- 1.5 lbs boneless, skinless chicken thighs

- 1/4 cup harissa paste

- 1/2 cup plain Greek yogurt

- 2 tablespoons olive oil

- 2 cloves garlic (minced)

- 1 teaspoon ground cumin

- 1 teaspoon ground coriander

- Salt and black pepper to taste

Instructions:

1. In a bowl, whisk together harissa paste, Greek yogurt, olive oil, minced garlic, ground cumin, ground coriander, salt, and black pepper to create the marinade.

2. Season chicken thighs with salt and black pepper.

3. Coat chicken thighs with the harissa yogurt marinade. Marinate for at least 30 minutes.

4. Preheat the grill to medium-high heat.

5. Grill chicken thighs for 5-7 minutes per side or until fully cooked.

6. Garnish with fresh cilantro before serving.

Essential Nutritional Information:

- Calories: 320 per serving

- Fat: 20g

- Carbohydrates: 5g

- Protein: 25g

Tips:

- Use full-fat Greek yogurt for creaminess.

- Serve with a side of couscous.

Tricks:

- Drizzle with extra harissa for added heat.

- Grill lemon wedges for a citrusy kick.

Ingredient Substitutions:

- Substitute harissa paste with red pepper flakes and smoked paprika.

- Use coconut yogurt for a dairy-free alternative.

Chili Lime Grilled Chicken Tacos

Summary: Spice up your taco night with Chili Lime Grilled Chicken Tacos. This recipe features marinated chicken thighs with a zesty chili lime flavor, served in warm tortillas with your favorite toppings.

Protein Content: Approximately 20 grams of protein per serving.

Ingredients:

- 1.5 lbs boneless, skinless chicken thighs

- Zest and juice of 2 limes

- 2 tablespoons olive oil

- 1 tablespoon chili powder

- 1 teaspoon cumin

- 1 teaspoon paprika

- 1/2 teaspoon garlic powder

- Salt and black pepper to taste

- Corn or flour tortillas

- Toppings: diced tomatoes, shredded lettuce, avocado, cilantro, lime wedges

Instructions:

1. In a bowl, mix lime zest, lime juice, olive oil, chili powder, cumin, paprika, garlic powder, salt, and black pepper to create the marinade.

2. Season chicken thighs with the chili lime marinade. Marinate for at least 30 minutes.

3. Preheat the grill to medium-high heat.

4. Grill chicken thighs for 5-7 minutes per side or until fully cooked.

5. Slice grilled chicken and assemble tacos with desired toppings.

Essential Nutritional Information:

- Calories: 300 per serving

- Fat: 15g

- Carbohydrates: 15g

- Protein: 20g

Tips:

- Char tortillas on the grill for extra flavor.

- Drizzle with lime crema for creaminess.

Tricks:

- Grill corn on the cob as a side dish.

- Make a salsa with grilled pineapple for sweetness.

Ingredient Substitutions:

- Substitute chili powder with chipotle powder for smokiness.

- Use lettuce wraps for a low-carb option.

Honey Mustard Glazed Grilled Chicken

Summary: Delight your palate with the sweet and tangy flavors of Honey Mustard Glazed Grilled Chicken. This recipe features chicken breasts glazed with a luscious honey mustard sauce, grilled to perfection.

Protein Content: Approximately 30 grams of protein per serving.

Ingredients:

- 1.5 lbs boneless, skinless chicken breasts

- 1/4 cup Dijon mustard

- 2 tablespoons honey

- 2 tablespoons whole grain mustard

- 1 tablespoon olive oil

- 2 cloves garlic (minced)

- Salt and black pepper to taste

Instructions:

1. In a bowl, whisk together Dijon mustard, honey, whole grain mustard, olive oil, minced garlic, salt,

and black pepper to create the honey mustard glaze.

2. Season chicken breasts with salt and black pepper.

3. Brush chicken breasts with the honey mustard glaze, reserving some for basting.

4. Preheat the grill to medium-high heat.

5. Grill chicken breasts for 6-8 minutes per side or until fully cooked, basting with the glaze.

6. Serve with extra honey mustard glaze on the side.

Essential Nutritional Information:

- Calories: 350 per serving

- Fat: 15g

- Carbohydrates: 10g

- Protein: 30g

Tips:

- Grill lemon wedges for a citrusy garnish.

- Pair with a crisp arugula salad.

Tricks:

- Grill peaches for a sweet side dish.

- Add a pinch of smoked paprika for depth.

Ingredient Substitutions:

- Substitute whole grain mustard with spicy brown mustard.

- Use maple syrup instead of honey for a different sweetness.

Balsamic Rosemary Grilled Chicken

Summary: Indulge in the aromatic flavors of Balsamic Rosemary Grilled Chicken. This recipe features chicken thighs marinated in a harmonious blend of balsamic vinegar and fresh rosemary, grilled to perfection.

Protein Content: Approximately 25 grams of protein per serving.

Ingredients:

- 1.5 lbs boneless, skinless chicken thighs

- 1/4 cup balsamic vinegar

- 2 tablespoons olive oil

- 2 tablespoons fresh rosemary (chopped)

- 2 cloves garlic (minced)

- Salt and black pepper to taste

Instructions:

1. In a bowl, mix balsamic vinegar, olive oil, chopped fresh rosemary, minced garlic, salt, and black pepper to create the marinade.

2. Season chicken thighs with salt and black pepper.

3. Coat chicken thighs with the balsamic rosemary marinade. Marinate for at least 30 minutes.

4. Preheat the grill to medium-high heat.

5. Grill chicken thighs for 5-7 minutes per side or until fully cooked.

6. Garnish with extra fresh rosemary before serving.

Essential Nutritional Information:

- Calories: 320 per serving

- Fat: 20g

- Carbohydrates: 5g

- Protein: 25g

Tips:

- Brush with extra balsamic glaze while grilling.

- Serve with roasted vegetables for a complete meal.

Tricks:

- Marinate chicken in a sealed plastic bag for even coverage.

- Baste with melted butter for added richness.

Ingredient Substitutions:

- Substitute balsamic vinegar with red wine vinegar.

- Use dried rosemary if fresh is not available.

Teriyaki Pineapple Grilled Chicken

Summary: Transport your taste buds to the tropics with Teriyaki Pineapple Grilled Chicken. This recipe features chicken breasts marinated in a sweet and savory teriyaki sauce, grilled to perfection, and topped with grilled pineapple slices.

Protein Content: Approximately 30 grams of protein per serving.

Ingredients:

- 1.5 lbs boneless, skinless chicken breasts
- 1/2 cup teriyaki sauce
- 1/4 cup pineapple juice
- 2 tablespoons soy sauce
- 2 tablespoons brown sugar
- 1 teaspoon ginger (minced)
- 2 cloves garlic (minced)
- Pineapple slices (for grilling)

Instructions:

1. In a bowl, whisk together teriyaki sauce, pineapple juice, soy sauce, brown sugar, minced ginger, and minced garlic to create the marinade.

2. Season chicken breasts with salt and black pepper.

3. Coat chicken breasts with the teriyaki pineapple marinade. Marinate for at least 30 minutes.

4. Preheat the grill to medium-high heat.

5. Grill chicken breasts for 6-8 minutes per side or until fully cooked.

6. Grill pineapple slices for 2-3 minutes per side.

7. Serve chicken with grilled pineapple slices on top.

Essential Nutritional Information:

- Calories: 350 per serving

- Fat: 15g

- Carbohydrates: 15g

- Protein: 30g

Tips:

- Reserve some marinade for brushing while grilling.

- Garnish with chopped cilantro for freshness.

Tricks:

- Grill red bell peppers alongside for color.

- Serve over a bed of coconut rice.

Ingredient Substitutions:

- Substitute brown sugar with honey.

- Use pineapple chunks if slices are not available.

Lime Cilantro Grilled Chicken Skewers

Summary: Elevate your grilling experience with Lime Cilantro Grilled Chicken Skewers. This recipe features marinated chicken skewers infused with zesty lime and fresh cilantro, grilled to perfection.

Protein Content: Approximately 25 grams of protein per serving.

Ingredients:

- 1.5 lbs boneless, skinless chicken thighs (cut into strips)

- Wooden skewers (soaked in water)

- Zest and juice of 2 limes

- 1/4 cup fresh cilantro (chopped)

- 2 tablespoons olive oil

- 2 cloves garlic (minced)

- Salt and black pepper to taste

Instructions:

1. In a bowl, mix lime zest, lime juice, chopped fresh cilantro, olive oil, minced garlic, salt, and black pepper to create the marinade.

2. Thread chicken strips onto soaked wooden skewers and place them in a shallow dish.

3. Pour the lime cilantro marinade over the chicken skewers, ensuring they are well coated. Marinate for at least 1 hour.

4. Preheat the grill to medium-high heat.

5. Grill the chicken skewers for 5-7 minutes per side or until fully cooked.

6. Garnish with extra fresh cilantro before serving.

Essential Nutritional Information:

- Calories: 320 per serving

- Fat: 15g

- Carbohydrates: 5g

- Protein: 25g

Tips:

- Baste with extra marinade while grilling.

- Serve over a bed of quinoa or couscous.

Tricks:

- Grill lime wedges for a citrusy touch.

- Use wooden skewers for easy serving.

Ingredient Substitutions:

- Substitute cilantro with parsley or mint.

- Use lemon if limes are not available.

Smoky Paprika Grilled Chicken Thighs

Summary: Delight in the rich and smoky flavors of Smoky Paprika Grilled Chicken Thighs. This recipe features succulent chicken thighs seasoned with a blend of smoky paprika and spices, grilled to perfection.

Protein Content: Approximately 25 grams of protein per serving.

Ingredients:

- 1.5 lbs boneless, skinless chicken thighs

- 2 tablespoons smoked paprika

- 1 tablespoon olive oil

- 1 teaspoon garlic powder

- 1 teaspoon onion powder

- 1/2 teaspoon cayenne pepper

- 1/2 teaspoon cumin

- Salt and black pepper to taste

Instructions:

1. In a bowl, mix smoked paprika, olive oil, garlic powder, onion powder, cayenne pepper, cumin, salt, and black pepper to create the spice rub.

2. Season chicken thighs with the smoky paprika spice rub, ensuring even coverage.

3. Preheat the grill to medium-high heat.

4. Grill chicken thighs for 5-7 minutes per side or until fully cooked.

5. Allow chicken to rest before serving.

Essential Nutritional Information:

- Calories: 320 per serving

- Fat: 20g

- Carbohydrates: 2g

- Protein: 25g

Tips:

- Serve with a side of grilled vegetables.

- Brush with olive oil before applying the spice rub.

Tricks:

- Grill lemon wedges for a citrusy garnish.

- Use a meat thermometer for accurate doneness.

Ingredient Substitutions:

- Substitute smoked paprika with regular paprika.

- Add a pinch of chipotle powder for extra smokiness.

Garlic Herb Butter Grilled Chicken

Summary: Indulge in the luxurious flavors of Garlic Herb Butter Grilled Chicken. This recipe features chicken breasts basted with a decadent garlic herb butter, grilled to perfection.

Protein Content: Approximately 30 grams of protein per serving.

Ingredients:

- 1.5 lbs boneless, skinless chicken breasts

- 1/2 cup unsalted butter (softened)

- 4 cloves garlic (minced)

- 2 tablespoons fresh parsley (chopped)

- 1 tablespoon fresh thyme leaves

- Salt and black pepper to taste

Instructions:

1. In a bowl, mix softened butter, minced garlic, chopped fresh parsley, fresh thyme leaves, salt, and black pepper to create the garlic herb butter.

2. Season chicken breasts with salt and black pepper.

3. Preheat the grill to medium-high heat.

4. Grill chicken breasts for 6-8 minutes per side or until fully cooked.

5. Baste the chicken with the garlic herb butter during the last few minutes of grilling.

6. Allow chicken to rest before serving, brushing with additional herb butter if desired.

Essential Nutritional Information:

- Calories: 350 per serving

- Fat: 20g

- Carbohydrates: 2g

- Protein: 30g

Tips:

- Use a compound butter for added flavor.

- Serve with roasted garlic mashed potatoes.

Tricks:

- Grill additional garlic cloves for a milder flavor.

- Top with a sprinkle of fresh herbs before serving.

Ingredient Substitutions:

- Substitute thyme with rosemary or oregano.

- Use ghee or olive oil for a healthier butter alternative.